# WANTAGE, FARINGDON
## & THE VALE VILLAGES
### IN OLD PHOTOGRAPHS

Brian

Wishing you a

Very Merry Christmas, 2004,

Love + best Wishes,

Tilly + Family.

x

THIS FAMOUS VIEW ACROSS THE VALE illustrates the advantage of the position of the nearby hillfort. The White Horse lies above his Manger, overlooking Dragon Hill, where St George slew the dragon. The spilled blood prevents grass growing on the spot, so goes the legend – one of many associated with the area. In fact, Dragon Hill was artificially levelled sometime in the past.

# WANTAGE, FARINGDON
## & THE VALE VILLAGES
## IN OLD PHOTOGRAPHS

COLLECTED BY

## NANCY HOOD

Budding
BOOKS

A Budding Book

First published in 1987 by Alan Sutton Publishing Limited

This edition published in 1998 by Budding Books,
an imprint of Sutton Publishing Limited
Phoenix Mill · Thrupp · Stroud · Gloucestershire GL5 2BU

A catalogue record for this book is available from the British Library

ISBN 1-84015-062-9

Typesetting and origination by
Sutton Publishing Limited.
Printed in Great Britain by
WBC Limited, Bridgend, Mid-Glamorgan.

# CONTENTS

THE LOYD LINDSAYS of the Lockinge Estate were the largest landowners in Berkshire. Lord Wantage was an MP and High Sheriff, playing an active role in both national politics and local affairs. Here the Provincial Grand Lodge of Berkshire Freemasons meet at Lockinge House, July 1900.

# INTRODUCTION

A traveller's view of this western part of the Vale of the White Horse is not so very different from that of John Leland, in the reign of Elizabeth I: from Oxford he found 'The ground was meatly wooddy ... thens 10 mils al by chaumpain and sum corne, but most pasture to Faringdon.' Towards Wantage by Hanney there was 'hilly ground well wooddid and fruitefull of corne ... by lovelle ground in sum partes marschy ... unto Wanetinge that standithe on the right ripe (bank) of a praty broke ...'

Both Wantage and Faringdon still lie in a predominantly agricultural landscape – a scene in which the details change while the overall impression is one of continuity. Where Leland noticed open field, woodland, pasture and low marshy ground, improvements in machinery, drainage and fertilisers in the last two hundred years have enabled more land to be turned to arable fields.

Some of this change has been recorded by the Victorian country photographer – but his camera takes us back only a little over a hundred years. Not until after 1910 did local newspapers use photographs extensively to enliven their columns of small print and adverts. The Kodak Brownie did much to fill the gap, early in this century, in family portraits, souvenir photographs and snapshots taken for the pure novelty of it. Through these photographs we can relate to the lives of the ordinary people who lived in our locality just before us, and see the changes in the town and countryside around them.

The chances are that, in a village of 500–700 people, a hundred years ago, everyone was working within a mile of so of his home. Settlement in the Vale of the White Horse developed in close relationship to the geology and structure of the clay vale and chalk and limestone hills. The Oxford clay of the Thames Valley, the limestone North Berks Ridge, the clays of the Vale proper, the greensand and chalk steps up the steep scarp slope, lie in broad bands running east–west. Each type of clay, sand and stone yields a characteristic soil which in turn determines what can be best grown, grazed or built on it.

Early man cleared the birch and pine woodlands of the chalk downs because his tools of stone and bone could tackle it; the first fields, the remains of which can still be seen at Knighton and Letcombe Downs, were on chalk. The oldest monument made by man in the area, Wayland's Smithy long barrow, was built on a pavement of sarsen stones cleared for fields over 5000 years ago. Later, iron tools enabled the heavier oak forest on the clay soils to be cleared and managed as coppices, fields and meadow.

Settlement then moved from the downs to the spring-line, formed where rain water soaking through the chalk hit marl or clay and burst to the surface. The spring-line, already followed by a lowland summer-road parallel to the Ridgeway, was settled at least by Roman times. Remains of villas or farmsteads have been found at Woolstone, Uffington, Baulking, Fawler, Challow, Stanford, Letcombe and Wantage, under the chalk scarp, and similarly on the northern limestone ridge from Faringdon to Cumnor. These villa estates would have had pasture on the uplands, spring water, meadow along the brooks and a loamy sandy soil in between for arable fields.

This pattern was taken over by Saxon settlers and these estates are some of the first to be recorded historically. The charters of the ninth century, which listed the boundaries of a property when it changed hands, survive for almost the whole of the Vale; in them are recorded the roots of the parish and village of today. The long strips of land, running at right angles to the ridges, have become known as 'strip parishes'. Their shape was determined by the need for a variety of soils for viable settlement: meadow for cows, land near the village for cornfields, orchards, a water supply, and upland pasture for sheep.

Markets developed around some of these manorial estates – the gift of the king as at Wantage, or the privilege of an abbey, as at Shellingford. The tolls and dues might make the fortunes of the local lord and the rights to fairs and markets were the source of many disputes. In 1276, a 50-year tussle between Fulk Fitzwaryn of Wantage and the Abbot of Abingdon over competing fairs resulted in the killing by Fulk's men of one Seman of Shellingford and strong-arm tactics to force the fair-goers to Wantage. Other medieval markets were at Shrivenham, Faringdon, Stanford, Baulking and East Hendred. There, in addition, two yearly cloth fairs stretched up the 'Golden Mile' from the village up the downs. The village feast on the saint's day of the dedication of the parish church is often a relic of these fairs.

By chance Wantage and Faringdon have been the survivors as market towns. Leland said that Faringdon, known as Cheping, or Market Faringdon, now had 'none or very small market' at that time. But at Faringdon there was an attempt to organise the growing town as a Borough by the thirteenth century – there were 51 long narrow burgage plots laid out along what is now London Road, and the medieval South Street, High Street, Gildon Street and Claypits. Those along London Road remain in the modern property boundaries, and together with the Market Place, Cornmarket and church, mark the heart of the medieval town.

The market was the focus of Wantage too, across the brook from the presumed centre of Roman occupation, near the parish church. The town remained a collection of four manors struggling under the administrative institutions of the feudal system, until the rights of the Lords of the Manor were finally purchased by the Town Commissioners in 1868. Some of the medieval closes leading from the Market Place survive in Wantage, where the encroachment of groups of shops on to the wide open Market Square is evident.

The two towns have contrasting buildings too: Faringdon's stone façades are said to be copies of the style of Coleshill House built c. 1650–62 for Sir George Pratt to designs by Inigo Jones. Otherwise it is honey-coloured ashlar or rubblestone quarried nearby, with stone tile roofs. Brick works, established in the mid-eighteenth century wherever clay and sand were conveniently to hand, provided materials for the modest expansion along the turnpike roads leading from the town.

Use of bricks can be seen more dramatically in Wantage, where the half-timbered gables of the Market Place were re-fronted immediately the new building material became available. Brickworks were at Uffington, Fernham, Faringdon, Eaton Hastings, Stanford, Childrey and even at Lockinge, on the downs.

With coal coming by canal (1810), and soon afterwards by rail (1840), brickmaking and other industries serving the farming villages around, such as agricultural engineering, milling, malting and brewing, took off. The countryside must have hummed with the noise of steam engines. Back in the villages the steam age did not empty the land for the towns as in the industrial north; populations doubled over the nineteenth century.

Farming, dairying and woodland management, or one of the many crafts and skills which supported the farmer, continued to provide employment. Blacksmiths, carpenters, wheelwrights, millers, thatchers, masons, shoemakers, tailors, bakers, publicans might all be found in a medium-sized village. Boys went to work in the fields, or perhaps took an apprenticeship which kept them out of trouble in virtually indentured labour for seven years; girls went into domestic service. The pattern changed not so much with steam and the Great War, as with the motor car engine and then the Second World War.

The second half of this century has seen the development of the towns and villages taken in hand by planners. It is the link between the people and the land that has been broken: the companies on the industrial estates do not necessarily relate to the products of the countryside and not so many people live and work in the same community. It is harder to keep the community working together. A look back through these old photographs, which document some of these changes up to 1974, may bring the past back into focus.

Nancy Hood
August 1987

NO ONE HAS REGRETTED THE LOSS OF THIS UGLY TOWN HALL, which lasted only 50 years before being removed to make way for the statue of Alfred the Great in 1877.

THE TOWN HALL which replaced it can be seen beyond the statue – a mock-Tudor style building occasionally said to be by G.E. Street, but this is doubtful.

The Market, Wantage.

THE SOUTH SIDE OF WANTAGE MARKET PLACE still has the Georgian façades, seen here in 1911.

ARBERY'S has hardly changed; here it is decorated for the Jubilee of 1935 – note the portraits of King George V and Queen Mary.

SHOPS MOVED PREMISES OFTEN – Belcher's moved from here on Church Lane to a site next to the Post Office. The last Belcher retired in 1983.

ONE OF THE OLDEST IRONMONGERS IN WANTAGE, Kent's shop is decorated for Queen Victoria's Jubilee in 1887.

ESTABLISHED OVER A CENTURY.

# Messrs. J. E. & F. Cottrell

### Purveyors of the finest quality
### ❦ BEEF and MUTTON. ❦

The Oldest Butchers' Establishment in the Town.

Specialities : { PRIME      CALVES HEADS,
PICKLED    SWEETBREADS,
TONGUES.    CORNED BEEF.

All Orders by Post will receive prompt attention.

❦ ❦ ❦

## Market Place, WANTAGE. Telephone No. 7.

THIS HALF-TIMBERED JETTIED SHOP was taken down in the 1950s, the beginning of the end for the north side of Wantage Market Place.

KATE EVANS AND EVE HARRIS stand outside their shop on Wantage Market Place, c. 1920.

WANTAGE STORES, c. 1926, was a single episode in 300 years of a grocer's business on this Market Place property.

THREE GENERATIONS OF HUGHES kept a shoemaker's shop in Wantage. Sidney Hughes, here with his sister in front of the shop on the Market Place, c. 1935, retired in the 1960s.

THE CHANGE TO READY-TO-WEAR SUPPLIERS had advantages with slick advertising.

BEHIND THE GEORGIAN FAÇADE lie gabled half-timbered buildings, some 300 years old. This was the former Crown of Old England, a coaching inn – note the covered carriageway.

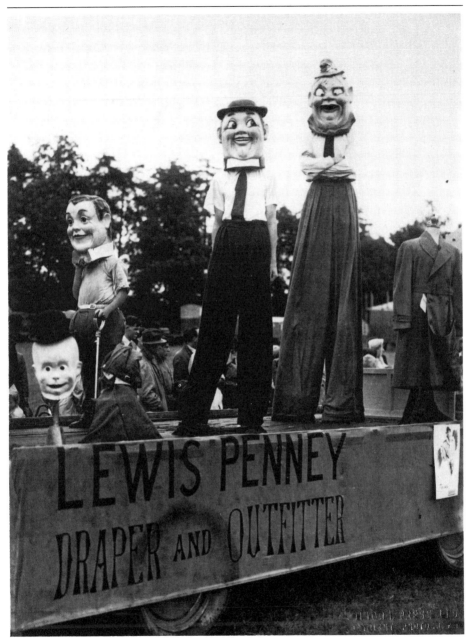

LEWIS PENNEY'S FLOAT at the 1954 Carnival advertises in a cheerful post-war atmosphere.

## BREWERS AND MALTSTERS,
## Wine and Spirit Merchants,
### — WANTAGE. —

**WINES OF EXCELLENT QUALITY AND 'SPECIAL' SPIRITS.**

PRICE LIST.

| | Per. Gall. | Per. Doz. |
|---|---|---|
| BOOTH'S GIN ... ... ... ... | 14 0 | ... 28 0 |
| OLD JAMAICA RUM ... ... | 16 0 | ... 32 0 |
| FINE COGNAC BRANDY, Pale & Brown | 28 0 | ... 56 0 |
| OLD IRISH WHISKY ... ... | 18 0 | ... 36 0 |
| OLD SCOTCH WHISKY ... | 18 0 | ... 36 0 |
| BRITISH BRANDY, Pale & Brown ... | 16 0 | ... 32 0 |
| PORTS, Fine Old and Tawny ... From | 24 0 to | 48 0 |
| SHERRIES, Fine Old Pale and Brown ,, | 24 0 to | 48 0 |
| CLARETS, ... ... ... ,, | 12 0 to | 24 0 |
| BURGUNDIES ... ... ... ,, | 24 0 to | 36 0 |

(Cognac Brandy, Old Irish Whisky, Old Scotch Whisky — Guaranteed 6 Years Old.)

CHAMPAGNE, all leading Brands at current prices.

DITTO, 'Vin d' Ay,' dry sparkling, 2/6, pint; 4/6, quart.

LIQUEURS: Cherry Brandy, Sloe Gin, Ginger Brandy, Ginger Gin, Orange Bitters, Peppermint, Cloves, &c.

---

### ALL GOODS DELIVERED FREE.
### ☞ FOR BEER PRICE LIST SEE OVER.

MARKET PLACE in 1895, with the Portwell given to the town in the sixteenth century by Sir Henry Unton.

MARKET PLACE, Faringdon, 1930s.

STAFF PHOTOGRAPHS were taken of Chamberlain's Grocers, Market Place, Faringdon, in 1909 and 1931.

FARINGDON'S SHEEP MARKET was in Market Place and the cattle market was on Church Street.

AT THE OTHER END OF FARINGDON'S HIGH STREET from the Market Place was the Corn Exchange, built in 1863.

THESE TWO VIEWS OF FARINGDON'S TOWN CENTRE show the seventeenth-century Market House before (1901) and after (1905) it began to be used as the Fire Station. The Crown, to the right, is of Elizabethan date, although it has been re-fronted many times.

ON LONDON STREET the closely packed shops reflect the medieval property boundaries, seen here in 1904 (above) and the 1930s (below).

HENRY ROBINS AND EDGAR ARGANT are in front of Ann's Garage, Marlborough Street, Faringdon, 1912.

MARLBOROUGH STREET is seen here in the 1930s.

OUTSIDE PARKER'S REFRESHMENT ROOMS, also Corn Stores, Baker and Confectioner on Marlborough Street, Faringdon, stand left to right: Mr Edington, Horace Hickman, J. Parker and Frank Wheeler in 1916.

GLOUCESTER STREET, Faringdon, 1895.

GRAVEL WALK, Faringdon, 1905.

THIS CROSSROADS IN FARINGDON is now almost unrecognisable as a busy roundabout, c. 1910.

Church Lane, Ashbury.

FROM CHURCH LANE, Ashbury, there is a view across the Vale of the White Horse.

SHRIVENHAM'S WIDE MAIN STREET was always a busy turnpike road, but who in the 30s would think it might need a by pass?

KENT'S ROW, GROVE, was owned by Kents, the Ironmongers, of Wantage. The thatched half was once a yeoman farm house, first extended, then divided into five cottages. Outside, on Main Street, stands Edgar Povey, who worked for the Railway, c. 1910. The cottages have now gone.

THE WHITE HORSE PUB, at Woolstone, is one of several in the area named after the chalk horse on the downs.

A PENNY STAMP sent this postcard from Kingston Lisle, showing the village shop and Post Office in 1919.

BUCKLAND'S STONE WALLS AND THATCHED COTTAGES are built with the coral ragstone of the North Berkshire Ridge.

THIS STONE-WALLED ROSE GARDEN is in Longworth.

STANFORD-IN-THE-VALE had three village greens; this is Church Green.

THERE IS A LONG VILLAGE STREET — note here the sun reflecting on the blue and red brickwork.

THE VILLAGE OF LETCOMBE BASSETT has a classic situation at the foot of the Downs, on the spring-line.

SELDOM WERE PEOPLE ABOUT IN THE VILLAGES; in Letcombe Regis here the trap and the haycart meet.

THE PLOUGH AT EAST HANNEY is now the Vintage Restaurant.

VILLAGERS STAND AROUND THE LITTLE GREEN at the crossroads, East Hanney, c. 1900 – a less than quiet spot today.

THE GREEN AT CHILDREY was the centre of village life – the pub, the Hatchet, was on the right, the pond in the centre and the wheelwright's on the left, c. 1899.

AN IRON BRIDGE crosses the Ock River at East Hanney.

WALLS MADE OF COB AND THATCH were once common in villages without a local supply of stone – a few survive at East Hendred.

ALL OF THE THATCHED ROOFS HAVE DISAPPEARED from this corner of Horn Lane and the road to the Downs at East Hendred.

THIS VIEW OF THE SQUARE, WATCHFIELD, is dated 1908 by the postmark.

AT CHILDREY, The Crown pub greeted the traveller along the hollow-way leading from the Downs.

AT THE VILLAGE PUMP, Letcombe Regis, is Alice Alder, standing with some of the village children; Louise Addis and Lil Wilmot sit together on the second step. 1904/5.

THE BAKER'S ARMS was on Uffington High Street, with Chapel Lane leading off, 1916.

GEESE STRUT ACROSS THE GOOSE GREEN at Goosey, in a scene which could be 200 years ago.

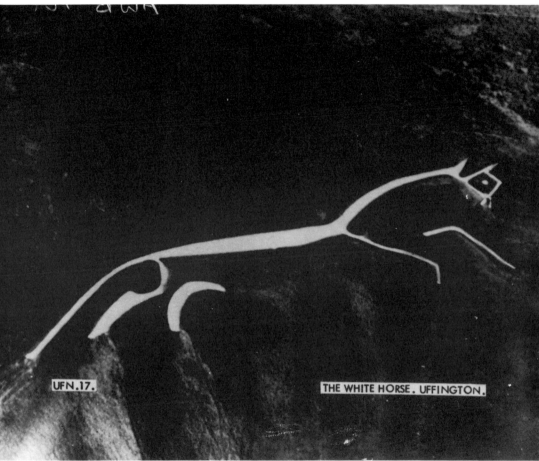

UFN.17.

THE WHITE HORSE. UFFINGTON.

CAN YOU SEE ANOTHER WHITE HORSE? Has it always been this shape? Some would say that erosion has changed the position of the legs and the width of the body. The Uffington horse is the oldest of all the white horses carved into the chalk, and probably dates from the late Iron Age.

WAYLAND'S SMITHY LONG BARROW truly resembled a cave in its tumbled-down state, prior to reconstruction in the 1960s. Legend has associated it with the gods and heroes of the Germanic homeland of the Anglo-Saxons – the angry smith who hurled stones at people and who worked at night. The tale of Weland the Smith is a bloodthirsty one of imprisonment, lust, murder and revenge.

RIGHT:
THE TOMB WAS EXCAVATED in 1962/3 and the great sarsen stones replaced upright; here a later ditch across the forecourt is being examined. Four of the original sarsen stones survived intact; the tallest is ten feet high and weighs four tons. Excavation determined its true function as a burial monument – in fact two barrows existed in the mound, each containing burials nearly 5000 years old.

Blowing Stone, Uffington

THE BLOWING STONE is in a former pub garden at Kingston Lisle. Children still try to re-create Alfred's trumpeting of victory over the Danes at Ashdown by blowing through the fossil root holes.

MATTHEW ARNOLD'S FYFIELD ELM was featured in his poem 'The Scholar Gipsy', written while at Oxford. It has since been felled.

MISS SIMMONDS stands by the isolated Pitchpoles Well at Letcombe, in a scene which shows the scrub woodland cover on the Downs before they came almost completely under the plough.

GREAT COXWELL TITHE BARN has always been a favourite subject for country photographer's rural scenes. This one was from Antonia of Swindon and Devizes. The barn, of Cotswold stone with a stone tile roof, dates from the thirteenth century and once held the produce of the grange farms of Beaulieu Abbey.

FARINGDON FOLLY, built by Lord Berner in 1935, is perhaps the last great folly built in England. It is 140 feet high and may be on the site of the twelfth-century fortifications of Stephen and Matilda.

THIS WING OF CHARNEY BASSETT MANOR is the solar and undercroft of a Norman manor house, once a grange farm of Abingdon Abbey. It is one of the best in the region, and dates from the thirteenth century.

FARINGDON HOUSE was built by Sir Henry Pye, Poet Laureate, 1780–5, and replaced an earlier enormous gabled manor.

KING'S MANOR, East Hendred, was one of five in this wealthy cloth-producing medieval village. Opposite stood the Pound, with stocks and pillory, and a small chantry chapel, now known as Champs Chapel.

A TRAGIC FIRE destroyed Coleshill House in 1952. It was thought to be the best Inigo Jones-inspired house of the mid seventeenth century in England, with a splendid staircase and plaster ceilings.

ASHDOWN HOUSE, built of chalk, was a rural escape from the plague for the first Earl of Craven, c. 1660. Much of its former surrounding forest with radiating avenues has gone, revealing the sarsen stones, 'grey wethers', in the park.

STYLES COTTAGE, Upper Common, Uffington, is really two cottages – the left side was built in the seventeenth century and the right side added later. In 1861 two farm labourers' families lived there, one with six children, one with nine; there are three rooms upstairs. It belonged to the Craven Estate.

THOMAS AND EMILY HERBERT stand in front of their Lockinge Estate cottage (c. 1930), a substantial seventeenth-century one which was not pulled down by the Loyd-Lindsays during their re-housing of the estate workers in the 1860s.

BEHIND THIS CHALK AND BRICK COTTAGE AT UFFINGTON can be seen the old fire station, 1916.

THIS TINY COTTAGE on a triangular piece of waste, Sheephouse Fields Cottage, with its pig-sty and chicken run, used to house agricultural labourers of the Longworth Estate. Later a family of hawkers lived there and called it 'Abingdon Villa'.

THESE MODEL ESTATE HOUSES belong to the Pusey Estate, and are almost adjacent to the House, Park and church.

G.E. STREET designed this gothic-style estate housing at Charney Bassett in 1852 – a small scale model village for the Pusey Estate.

THESE COTTAGES IN HANNEY AND SPARSHOLT, condemned in the 1960s, show what dark and crowded lives lay behind our view of life in the country.

THIS TERRACE WAS BUILT FOR THE CANAL WHARF AT GROVE, which lay on the other side. They have been virtually rebuilt, but left to right, they are Wharf Cottage, the Carpenter's, the Boatman's, the Stable and Blacksmith's.

NEW HOUSING AT GROVE illustrates the pressure on the villages which comes with new jobs on the industrial estates and research centres in the market towns. Once a hamlet, Grove now approaches Wantage in population. So far though, amenities have not kept pace.

White Horse Hill. Uffington.

HORSE-DRAWN PLOUGHS sit in the field below the manger, overlooked by the White Horse.

View from The Ridgeway. Letcombe Bassett.

THE COUNTRY PHOTOGRAPHER has found an obliging real white horse in the Vale.

NOTE THE VARIETY OF MEADOW FLOWERS IN THE HAYFIELD at Letcombe. Everyone turned out for the hay harvest, but now it is mowed quickly by tractor.

ON THE HORSE-DRAWN REAPER BINDER at West Hendred, are Bill Seares, Fred Roberts and his mother Patty Roberts, 1920–30.

THE STEAM ENGINE here at Wier Farm, East Hanney, came from Dandridge's Mill, 1900–1910. Bobby Ford is threshing with the Eadys on their farm.

THE COMBINE HARVESTER, seen here at Fernham, needs but one operator.

VALE FARMS were formerly mainly dairy farms – famous for cheeses in the shape of hares and pineapples, and of a single-Gloucester type. Milk production replaced butter and cheesemaking in the nineteenth century, when it could easily be sent by train. Here cows still graze upon Grove Green, 1910.

SHEEP ARE PASTURED ON THE DOWNS ABOVE LETCOMBE; the water barrel is an improvement over the dew pond.

G. TYLER was shepherd at Letcombe. The sheep are of a Down variety, less common today.

RADCOT BRIDGE was one of the traditional sheep-washing places along the river – this scene was in 1885.

MR HERBERT, whose cottage appears on p.61, surveys a field of giant mangels at Lockinge, around 1900. These were introduced into England in the early eighteenth century to improve winter fodder for sheep.

DOUGLAS EADY, aged 10, whose father also worked on the Estate, was caught by the photographer in the same field at Lockinge.

A FAMILY SNAPSHOT is taken while the hay rick is being thatched, *c.* 1930, at Lockinge.

A PHOTOGRAPH ALBUM from Letcombe Regis manor is unusual in having many snapshots of the farm labourers. Here are A. Morris and E. Francis outside the house, and Mr S. Kent with the shire-horses, opposite.

BEEHIVES IN THE KITCHEN GARDEN at Letcombe ensure pollination of the fruit trees as well as a honey supply.

IN CHILDREY the Smiths owned the traction engine to be hired out to farmers, left to right: Arthur Smith junior, Arthur Smith senior, Frank Edmonds (driver), a carpenter, Jim Preston, Mr Preston senior, boy from Little (West) Challow.

MR W. STONE, blacksmith, hammers a horseshoe at the Harrison's Forge at East Hendred, 1926. This village, like many, had several smithies to deal with the making and repair of agricultural implements as well as shoeing horses.

HARRISON'S ABANDONED FORGE AND WHEELWRIGHT'S SHOP is the consequence of the change from horse-drawn wagons and equipment to tractors. The tyring kiln and huge sarsen stone tyring ring are still there, all waiting to be turned into a village museum.

NALDER AND NALDER ENGINEERING COMPANY at East Challow employed around 200 men at the turn of the century. The business began by making ploughs, threshing machines and portable steam engines for the local market, but added sieving and grading machines for malt, cocoa and coffee beans, which were shipped all over the Empire. Their malt-grading machines can still be seen in remote distilleries in Scotland.

APPRENTICESHIPS WERE FOR SEVEN YEARS. During the war, local women worked there on munitions and some found they preferred the work to domestic service. But the jobs went back to the lads afterwards.

THE BRICKWORKS AT BOW, Stanford-in-the-Vale, used sand and clay dug on the site, but there is nothing left of these works today.

THE BRICKWORKS AT UFFINGTON supplied bricks for repairing labourers' cottages and a spate of speculative building on the fringes of Faringdon and Wantage. This engine house survived for agricultural use after the works closed between the wars.

SWAN LANE, FARINGDON, home of Westall's Bakery – the ovens are still there. Photographed in 1979.

BILL LAY'S VILLAGE BAKERY at East Hanney was still going strong in the 1930s. Rose Cross holds the cottage loaf with Fred Carr in the hat; Mr Lay is on the right.

THE BAKER OF WEST HENDRED, F.H. Goodey, delivered bread by pony and trap to Ardington.

YOU HAVE TO GET UP EARLY TO SEE RACEHORSE TRAINING ON THE DOWNS; they are back in the stables for breakfast.

THE MILL AT LETCOMBE REGIS is typical of the manorial mills to which all the village corn was taken.

ranford-in-the-Vale.
S216

Fred. C. Palmer.
Swindon

THE MILL AT STANFORD-IN-THE-VALE is now a private house.

WILLOUGHBY'S MILL in Wantage belonged to the Manor of Priorshold, and probably existed at the time of the Domesday survey. Next to the mill was the Victorian Mill Cottage, where the Willoughbys lived. The mill was working until between the wars.

DANDRIDGE'S MILL at Hanney was a large operation for a village; steam engines and threshing machines were available for hire to local farmers.

The Mill, Wantage.

OPPOSITE THE ENTRANCE TO THE WHARF AT WANTAGE is Clark's Mill; this is the new mill building of c. 1912 which now uses electrically operated machinery. The old stone rollers were kept (and used until recently) in the old mill building on the opposite side of the mill stream. It is a going concern today, selling flour to both local customers and further afield, but the corn ground now is mostly French or Canadian.

Watercress Beds. Letcombe Bassett.

WATERCRESS was grown in most of the spring-line villages, from Ashbury to Blewbury, and shipped daily in season to London. Letcombe's watercress beds are seen best from this bridge over the Brook.

LESLIE TUBB OF LETCOMBE is the last watercress grower of the spring-line villages; he was almost put out of business by the drought of 1976.

MATTHEW REA'S CRESS BEDS at Stowell in Childrey were in use until the 1950s; Pike's Cottage is in the background.

EVERY PARISH HELPED ITS POOR IN SOME WAY through charity administered by its Overseers. These old Parish Rooms in Grove were converted from cottages let to the poor before Grove joined the Wantage Union in 1836. After that the poor had the advantage of Wantage's Workhouse. The cottages were used as a school, and then Parish Rooms, until taken down to build a new Village Hall.

THE FIRE ENGINE used the village pond here in Childrey at the fire on Easter Sunday 1932, which began in the barn, or bakery, of Mr Legge, who was also the postmaster. It destroyed the Post Office and many of the Parish Records kept there.

THESE ALMSHOUSES AT BOURTON are built of the local rag-stone.

THE COVENTRY ALMSHOUSES, Childrey, were opened in 1911 and cost £600. They were for women only, as there were already Fettiplace Almshouses for men and married couples.

A SERIES OF PUBLICITY PHOTOGRAPHS was taken in 1946 for the new Health Service to illustrate improved conditions for the elderly in the new Longworth Hospital. Many had come from Downs Hospital, Wantage, the former Workhouse.

ARMY MANOEUVRES
ORD ROBERTS
WITH LADY WANTAGE
AT WATCHFIELD.

LORD ROBERTS GREETS LADY WANTAGE during army manoeuvres at Watchfield, 1909. The message on the postcard noted that he disliked having his picture taken, but nevertheless agreed to this one.

THIS RED CROSS SEWING PARTY was part of the war effort, 1914–1918, in East Hanney.

THE CANNING UNIT OF EAST HANNEY, with Miss Andrewartha and Mrs Stevens, celebrates VE Day in 1945.

SUPPLY WAGONS wait in Wantage Market Place for loading and transport to the station, 1914–18.

FROM THE NEARBY CAMP AT SHRIVENHAM these army manoeuvres were a common sight.

THIS WATER CISTERN in Faringdon Market Place served the Army during World War II, seen here in a record photograph of 1945.

LEWIS NORTHCOTE practises haymaking with his nanny at East Hendred, c. 1910.

THE CHALK SCHOOL AT UFFINGTON, built in 1617, featured in *Tom Brown's School Days* by Thomas Hughes. Now it is the village museum. Behind it is Jenkins' blacksmith shop, 1916.

BOYS FROM THE SCHOOL AT UFFINGTON work on the allotment gardens, 1910.

THIS GROUP AT THE CHURCH SCHOOL, Watchfield, dates from 1908.

Ashbury School.

ASHBURY SCHOOLCHILDREN were summoned from class to decorate this country view.

THE NATIONAL SCHOOL on Stanford Road, Faringdon, was built in 1825. The land was given by Mr David Bennett, and it cost one penny a week to attend.

MANY MARKET TOWNS HAD A FEMALE SCHOOL OF INDUSTRY, as here on London Street, Faringdon, founded in 1833.

THIS LITTLE SCHOOLHOUSE replaced the 1526 Elizabethan school house in Childrey. It was built in 1732 by Sir George Fettiplace and his coat of arms can be seen on the gable end. It was in use as a school unit in 1913. Only the end wall with the foundation plaque remains; the school house roof fell into disrepair in spite of Sir John Betjeman's efforts to preserve it.

THE VILLAGE SCHOOL OF LETCOMBE BASSETT is a W. Butterfield design, c. 1870.

AT THE VILLAGE SCHOOL OF LETCOMBE REGIS in 1909, many family names of long standing occur: Palmer, Wilkins, Sims, Goodall, Alder, Froude, Goddings, Addis; some names will be found on the village war memorial.

ST MARY'S SCHOOL, WANTAGE, was founded by the Revd W.J. Butler, for the education of daughters of gentlemen, clergy and professional men. It was staffed by Sisters of the Convent of St Mary, which he also founded. This class is of the 1880s.

THE CLASS OF 1907 of the Church of England primary school in Wantage, brought their toys into this school photograph. Mr H.J. Ireson kept this picture.

MOST VILLAGE SCHOOLS PRACTISED THE MAYPOLE DANCE, as here at Uffington in 1916.

ANOTHER DANCE PRACTISED AT THE MAY DAY CELEBRATIONS is this stick dance, which has obvious links with the Morris Dance. This is at East Hanney School, c. 1910.

THE BOY SCOUT CAMP AT LONGWORTH was the outcome of a friendship between Lt. Col. Granville Walton of the Manor and Lord Baden Powell, founder of the Scout Movement. This meeting was in 1913.

THE GUIDES SOON FOLLOWED THE SCOUTS IN WANTAGE — this is the First King Alfred's Troop photographed by Tom Reveley in 1922. Guide leaders were: centre row, third left, Miss Eileen Adkin (Commandant), fourth left, Miss Olive Griswood, fifth left, Miss Minnie Hughes.

Old Berkshire Hounds at the L

THE COUNTRY PUB WAS OFTEN THE LOCAL SOCIAL CENTRE — here the Old Berkshire Hounds meet at the Lamb and Flag, Longworth. The date on the postcard is 1912.

THIS GROUP OF COURSING ENTHUSIASTS were assembled at Kingston Bagpuize House, home of Mr E.A. Strauss, the Liberal MP in 1906/7. William Jarvis, the boy whose face peers out between the shoulders of two men holding the greyhounds on the front row, remembers the scene well. Many Wantage families are represented: at the top Mr Granger, bank manager; mounted, right, Mr Hanks, the vet, and left, Mr Collard. Next to him, holding the 'slips' is Alf Sansum of the Greyhound pub, Letcombe Regis. John Arbery, the draper, stands by the window's lower right corner, near the elderly Mr Nicholls, the stationer. The lady in the centre, with a scarf tied around her hat, is the wife of the photographer, Tom Reveley; behind her and to the right is Mr Jarvis' mother and Arthur Belcher.

THIS TURN-OF-THE-CENTURY POLITICAL MEETING on Uffington Common attracted people from nearby villages also.

'LIVING BRIDGE' was performed at the Faringdon Flower Show in July 1906.

THE FIFE AND DRUM BAND was founded and led by bandmaster A.V. Gibbs, standing, second from right. They met at the King Alfred's Head pub, but there was no drinking, smoking or swearing.

THE LONGWORTH CLUB met at the Lamb and Flag, and were photographed by Henry Taunt.

LOCALS SIT OUTSIDE THE HARE AT WEST HENDRED, with Mr and Mrs Frank Quartermain. Left to right: Mrs Quartermain, W. Saunders, Frank Quartermain, (seated); Goddard, –?–, –?–, Roberts (standing), –?–, G. Stater (standing), E. Welsh (seated), Shepherd, J. Castle (standing), T. Castle (seated), Mulford (standing), K. Roberts (seated), –?–, B. Harries, c. 1910.

FRED MULFORD poses outside the Hare, now tile-hung, in the 1930s.

THE ABINGDON TRADITIONAL MORRIS DANCERS perform at Faringdon in 1939. The Mayor of Ock Street was Henry Hemmings, the musician was Harry Thomas and the Hornbearer was Jack Hyde.

MEMBERS OF THE WANTAGE AND DISTRICT FIELD CLUB inspect the building site on Littleworth Hill
– finds of Roman pottery and coins over the years indicated Roman settlement there, and
excavations took place over the next year 1973/74. Left to right: Mrs Jean Naish, Mrs Jean
Banford, Miss Kathleen Philip, Dr Thomas Ridsdill-Smith.

CRICKET was introduced at King Alfred's School, Wantage, in the 1870s.

WANTAGE TOWN FOOTBALL CLUB in 1909. Back, left to right: W.A. Noble, Secretary; F. Hankins, G. Shorey, A. Johnson, A. Burcel (linesman). Front, left to right: M. Hiskins, A. Bunce, W. Pierpoint.

THE CYCLING CLUB met at the Bear and had Lord Wantage as its President for many years.

AT WANTAGE, celebrations for the Coronation in 1911 took place at Stirlings Field, watched by this crowd of lovely hats.

THE COURTYARD OF STILES ALMSHOUSES, Wantage, is decorated for the coronation of King George V and Queen Mary, 1911.

SCENES FROM THE WANTAGE CARNIVAL held to celebrate peace in 1919. Nobly Chapman is the clown seated on the right (opposite, top). The football says 'Peace 1919'.

BILL DENNIS IN THE TIE AND LESLIE HUGHES IN THE CAP stand behind the chef at the Coronation Ox Roast in 1937, Wantage Market Place.

THIS WEDDING PARTY took place near Kingston Lisle in 1900, a photograph kept by Mr Taylor, whose uncles and mother are the children in the front row.

THIS SOMBRE VICTORIAN FAMILY LIVED AT FRAMLANDS, on the edge of Wantage in the 1880s. The father is Judge Makonochie.

HARPER, THE WIERKEEPER OF RADCOT, is seen in an early Henry Taunt photograph of the 1870s.

MISS LAVINIA SMITH of Downside, East Hendred, made a private museum of local agricultural equipment and bygones. At her death, in the 1950s, the collection went to the Museum of English Rural Life at Reading.

THE PHOTOGRAPHER TOM REVELEY OF WANTAGE is usually remembered for his country scenes and family portraits, but this is a wonderful, informal portrait study.

THE FIRST MRS SILVER of the Manor, Letcombe Regis, was known to drive into Wantage with her pet lion in the back seat of her open car.

THE ROUND HOUSE AT HINTON WALDRIST is one of the most well-known turnpike toll houses on the Oxford–Swindon road. A stone quarry lay behind it.

A BERKSHIRE WAGON, drawn by shire horses with their harness brasses gleaming, carries corn at Buckland.

THE FERRY ACROSS THE RIVER THAMES AT DUXFORD, Hinton Waldrist, must have been an uncomfortable experience from 1827–1920.

UFFINGTON WAS A BUSY PLACE, with a rail station, canal wharf, several smiths and wheelwrights, a malthouse and brickworks. The bridge over the canal, hoist and wharf lie behind the house, seen here in 1916.

BRIDGE COTTAGE, also on the Canal, lay at Knighton Turn, Uffington, 1916. The Wilts and Berks Canal opened in 1810 and linked the Vale of the White Horse from the Thames at Abingdon to Semington in Wiltshire, near Swindon.

THE HISKINS FAMILY ran the Wharf at Wantage – the house where they lived is in the background – built of stone brought by the canal 1810–20. The Wharfinger's house and the stable can still be seen near the filled-in Wharf basin off Mill Street.

THE WHARF at the town end of the Wantage Arm of the Wilts and Berks Canal became grown over soon after traffic ceased around 1900. The terrace opposite, Wharf Terrace, once a lively group of houses and a pub, gradually became derelict and was taken down in the early 70s.

THE WANTAGE ARM linked the Wharf with the main Wilts and Berks Canal two miles away, at Grove.

PINMARSH BRIDGE took the road over the Canal between Lockinge and Ardington.

GROVE TOP LOCK, with its lock-keeper's cottage, was one of a flight of seven through the village, which also had its own wharf. This was around 1900, when the life of the Canal was nearly over.

FROM 1864 FARINGDON HAD A BRANCH LINE TO UFFINGTON STATION on the main Great Western Railway line which opened in 1840. This photograph dates from 1919.

WANTAGE ROAD STATION was still equipped with old broad gauge track up until 1919.

A DONKEY AND TRAP takes the ladies to Wantage from the Manor at Letcombe.

HERE IS AN AFFECTIONATE LOOK AT THE WANTAGE TRAMWAY, one of several circulating at the time. The donkey laughing away is probably Arthur Hitchcock's 'moke' who reputedly won a race with the tram.

THE WANTAGE TRAMWAY opened in 1875; the office on Mill Street was given a new red brick facing in 1904. The line linked Wantage with Wantage Road Station on the Great Western Railway 2½ miles to the north. Apart from locals travelling on the GWR the biggest customers were for the good service: Clark's Mill, Weedons Coal, Wantage Engineering Company.

THE TOWN TERMINUS and passenger platform were behind the Mill Street offices; now the shed is bricked up for storage and garages.

THE GOODS YARD WAS NEXT TO THE WHARF; the lifting crane you can see was purchased from the Canal Company, after the canal closed.

DRIVER WEAVING AND TRAMWAY STAFF pose with Engine No. 7, the Manning Wardle Saddle Tank.

AT GROVE BRIDGE there was a passing loop, but the line crossed the turnpike road ungated. The whistle warned motor traffic of its approach, but was hardly necessary with the small number of cars on the country road. The most frequent accidents were derailments due to the condition of the track.

THE LAST ENGINE IN SERVICE WAS *SHANNON*, known locally as *Jane*, seen here on a siding at Wantage Road Station in 1948, after closure of the Tramway Company.

WITH *JANE,* ENGINE NO. 5, are Mr Widridge, signalman, and Mr Powell (with the hat) the station master, after restoration of the engine at the Swindon works. *Jane* is now at the Great Western Railway Museum at Didcot, where she can occasionally be seen in steam.

THE FIRST MOTOR IN WANTAGE was owned by Mr L. Pates; he also provided traction for the steam fire engine. Here he is driving with Mr F. Brooks in 1906.

THE WI OF EAST HANNEY take a charabanc outing in the mid 1920s. The omnibus made such outings, usually to seaside towns, accessible to many more people – but the day might begin at 6 a.m. as it took four hours to reach Southampton.

THE CHOIR PARTY TO BOURNMOUTH FROM EAST HANNEY, July 1923: Mr Noon, vicar; Mr Clinch, sexton; Mr Edwards, Headmaster. On the charabanc: C. Higgs, F. Bunce, G. Tombs, R. Breakspear, J. Bunce, E.H.W. & C. Cox, F. Daubney, V. Lamble, G. Burnett, G. Belcher, E. Cowie, F. Monk, J. Adams, D. Barrett, C. Barrow, J. Broughton, L. Clinch, W. Spinloe.

THE OMNIBUS CALLS IN AT THE ROSE AND CROWN, ASHBURY. This service made shopping in the market towns easier for country people; it opened up town and city jobs and marked the beginning of real suburban life.

WHO WOULD HAVE THOUGHT THAT THE COMING OF THE MOTOR CAR WOULD LEAD TO THIS in the 50 years that separate these two photographs? A demonstration for a bypass for Faringdon holds up a lorry in the Market Place, December 1972.

# ACKNOWLEDGEMENTS

Abingdon Museum • Mrs Akers • Mrs O. Ashthorpe • Miss S. Baker
Mrs J. Banford • Berkshire Archaeological Society • Mr A. W. Bourne
Mr D. Bradbrook • Miss C. Bradford • Mrs A. C. Castle • Mrs P. Childerley
Mrs J. Clayton • Mr J. Collier • Mrs M. Crook • Mr W. Dennis • Mr N. Eady
Mrs Eltham • Mr M. E. Eyre • Mr R. Fairfull • Mrs C. B. Fewins
Mr W. Fuller • Mr A. H. Gregory • Mr W. Hiskins • Mr T. Hook
Mr L. Hughes • Mrs S. Hughes • Mr H. J. Ireson • Mr R. James
Mr W. Jarvis • Mrs Lewis-Price • Mr J. Loftin • Mrs J. Loudon
Miss E. Lovegrove • Mr M. Murfett • National Monuments Record
Oxfordshire County Libraries • Oxford Mail and Times
Oxfordshire Museums Service • Oxford Publishing Company • Mrs L. Pates
Penny's Menswear • Miss K. Philip • Miss M. Powell • Reading Museum
Mrs W. Silver • Mr F. B. Simkins • Mrs J. Smith • Dr R. Squires
Mr W. Stanley • Swindon Museum • Mr Taylor • Mrs Theobold
Vale and Downland Museum Centre, Wantage

Wherever possible the original donor or lender of a photograph has been
acknowledged. Those from the various institutions and museums, after all,
represent many individual donations. Another invaluable contribution has
been the help in identifying and dating the photographs, and providing
background information, often from personal memory, which has been so
freely given by colleagues, owners and lenders. I should particularly like to
thank Daphne Jones for her help in assembling the material and Sue Etchells
for typing it.

Nancy Hood
October 1987